CONTACT THE AUTHOR

Mountainbird's books are available online wherever fine books are sold. Also, find them at selected bookstores including Pomegranate Books and Barnes & Noble in her hometown of Wilmington, North Carolina.

Other books include the creative memoir of true adventures from around the globe, *Lookin' Up in Down Times: Stars Shine Bright on a Moonless* Night and the inspirational children's picture book, *The Healing Circle,* illustrated by Gina Hagan.

Available in hardcover, paperback and e-book is this collection of 36 poems, *Mountainbird Melodies: Book One—Dances with Waterfalls*, by Mountainbird and illustrated by Lydia Noble, both of Wilmington, North Carolina. If you would like an autographed copy of this and any other book, order directly from Mountainbird. Or, mail your purchased copy to the author. At your request, she will return it autographed. Mailing costs apply.

Dear Reader,

May these quiet melodies help you navigate your own life and transform into **Fullness**. *May you discover beauty as you journey through your own life adventures.*

I'd love to hear from you. Submit queries, responses, or requests for workshops, talks, books, notes, or autographed gift copies to this email: mountainbirdauthorandartist@gmail.com

Mountainbird Melodies

Book One—Dances with Waterfalls

Poetry by Mountainbird

Illustrations by Lydia Noble

Copyright & Credits

GIVING THANKS

Thank you, first and foremost, Lord,

For carrying me even when I did not realize it.

Thank you, my sons and your father, for the

Treasures of memories, the happy ones, and even

The sad ones that make joy more precious.

Thank you, family, friends, romantic loves,

And acquaintances who shared moments,

Tough and, sometimes, tender.

Thank you all for loving me through the **Cocoon**

Of bitterness and grief.

For your patience during the times of **Awakening**

And onward to the **Fullness** of womanhood.

Thank you, each and every one of you,

For tears, laughter, shared stories, and faith

That made—and make—it possible to move onward

And upward.

The Lord your God is among you; He is mighty to save. He will rejoice over you with gladness; He will quiet you with His love, He will rejoice over you with singing.

Zephaniah 3.17 *Holy Bible*. (BSB).

DEDICATION

To my three sons

who made it possible for me to enjoy motherhood,

Anthony, Demetrius & Nicholas Falbo

. . .And clasped in my heart, the glorious sun-moon-star-jewel of
Each newborn gaze of my three sons.

Excerpt from *Jewels of Memory* by Mountainbird

CONTENTS

INTRODUCTION

Dear Reader,

May the kaleidoscope of moments found in *Mountainbird Melodies: Book One—Dances with Waterfalls* resonate with you and inspire you to grow emotionally and spiritually—no matter what stage or age of womanhood—whether in or out of the home, while working, writing, drawing, painting, or dancing through this amazing adventure we call *Life*.

My entrance into writing was reading and, much later, journaling. Reading avidly as a child, I focused on the story so deeply that, while reading, I would not even hear my parents calling. In college, twenty-page handwritten letters home became my norm.

After the end of a twelve-year marriage, I used a dream journal to uncover personal internal conflicts and discover a future vision. While bringing up my beloved three sons, I reflected on the tumultuous teenage times with private journal writing. In transitioning from a lonely and, often depressed, young adult to a more mature version of myself, my greatest source of help came from experiencing solace—and even joy—whenever I saw God in the sunshine, blue skies, the clouds, and the rain on long walks in nature.

Years later, as I reread my journal musings, words spilled over like a waterfall splashing the pages with poems. Still, I tentatively tiptoed into communicating my innermost thoughts and feelings with others. Out of love for Pastor LaVerne Anderson, my spiritual dad, I wrote, rewrote, and recited aloud my poem over and over all night long. The very next day, on his 80th birthday celebration, I presented the poem, "The Healing Circle," in front of about one hundred people! That marked my public debut as a writer. Thirty years later, this poem inspired a children's picture book of the same name, *The Healing Circle*.

Mountainbird Melodies

Book One—Dances with Waterfalls

Poetry by Mountainbird

Illustrations by Lydia Noble

COCOON

1   Instant Anything

What?

No instant anything

To take away this pain?

No cure for this dreary void?

No love to embrace, enfold, enjoin?

2   January

Heartache cries like a babe in the January night.

Dark is cold to the bone.

Snow freezes lingering loneliness.

No woodland quiet contemplation now.

Just lonely, leaden moan.

Hope wanes with winter's fading dusk.

But the next morning,

Can the heart sing in the dawning light?

3   Bowl Full of Cherries

Life is. . .

A mouth full of marbles,

A fist full of squid,

A belly full of triplets,

A head full of dynamite,

And a heart filled with goodbyes.

4   *Someday* and *Maybe*

Someday and *Maybe* are quietly killing me.

Yes moves across like a lightening shock.

I love you soothes like gliding on still summer waters.

While *Someday* and *Maybe* continue to stalk their prey.

I miss you offers little gasps of air.

You're wonderful seals a small smile of relief.

Someday and *Maybe* steal in with doom's delay.

You deserve the best whispers a fleeting hope.

I can't give it to you though chokes the final breath.

Someday and *Maybe* are quietly killing me.

5   Circles

Life goes 'round in circles.

Around and around the merry-go-round,

Music, bland circular motion

Amidst a relaxing carnival bliss.

Whirlpools of sorrow.

Alice cried a river of tears,

Swirled 'round and 'round,

Nearly drowned in her own despair.

Roller skaters dance in circles.

Continuous tedious circles,

Some attempt a backward advance,

A roller-ride going nowhere.

Why not a down-hill world

Where everything is effortless?

If we were riding bikes,

We'd always want downward hills.

Yet the hills, too, become circles.

Up, then down, return, and go upward again.

Isn't the earth a giant circle?

It's not just a downhill ride.

Dancers moving in a circle offer a ray of hope

Joy in music and movement lifts the spirit.

If we can dance in a circle, can't we live in a circle?

One happy circle. NO! It's a learning circle.

Strive like Sisyphus,

Roll that heavy rock,

Only to have it slip and have to roll it up again.

Perhaps, we progress inch by inch.

Solace in the winter night, where are you?

*Sisyphus (or Sisyphos) is a figure from Greek mythology who, as king of Corinth, became infamous for his general trickery and twice cheating death. He ultimately got his comeuppance when Zeus dealt him the eternal punishment of forever rolling a boulder up a hill in the depths of Hades. [www.ancient.eu]

6   Fear of Flying

You catch me in your whirlwind.

Fear and excitement embrace.

You take me to faraway spaces,

You spin me around again and again,

Until I'm so dizzy, I'm breathless.

Oh, do I make you high?

You transport me higher.

Yet, I have a fear of heights;

I'm afraid of falling.

If I overcome my fear and let go,

Will it be like a dream?

And then I'll fly higher?

My heart aches to soar with you;

But my head shouts, *Caution!*

You readily jump across the abyss, and land unscathed,

But, will I?

7   Wooing Wind

Wooing wind

Whispers in my wings,

Wishshshsh, and it will be.

8   Beckoning Beyond

The mountains beckon, echoing, *We are here*. She sifts through the ashes and peers through the blinding haze.

Like a border refugee thirsty in the Arizona desert, she walks weary in July's withering heat.

Sunset peeks through like the first glow of a blazing flash fire that will consume the parched grassland.

Like a nomad in a strange region, gingerly, she steps, searching for the narrow path on the dusty, grey earth.

That night, the full moon haunts, haunts, like the call to serve.

Yearning for the rush of the pulsating waterfall dripping, hitting, flowing over her from head to neck, back and arms. And down to and through her toes.

After her cool cleansing, her yawning comes before a deep slumber,

From which she awakens far beyond the desert plain

In a distant land, where she is gliding past palm trees that line the shore, on a boat softly pushing through the mirrored, ribbon river,

While she glides slowly, slowly, onward toward her mountain destiny.

9 Stars in the Night

Stars in the night that shine so bright.

Ventures so new. *I can do all with You!*

Thank You! for loving me and setting me free.

With You, precious is the life,

Where You take away all strife.

Even when faced with a giant test,

In You, I can find deep rest.

I take challenges, with You at my side.

Taking a deep breath, I open my arms wide,

With faith that You will always stay

Right with me, each and every day,

Thank You, Lord!

AWAKENING

10   By a New Salem Brook at Midwinter's Thaw

Singing waters caress my soul,

A gentle breeze fans my heart,

Blue sky colors my mind clear,

While soft earth massages winter-weary feet.

Lacking nothing now: I am whole

And, for this moment, at peace with the world;

For singing waters have caressed my soul.

11 The Potter's Dance

Uncertain, my hands brush the pliable clay.

Yet, I become bolder as I push,

pull,

smooth,

hug,

and wish.

I dance into a hole that almost reaches the bottom.

The form and I take a slow carousel ride.

I climb on and dream,

Discovering the Master's will.

I rest,

Tilt my head back, smile and

Peer into the dusk

Of a newly formed vessel.

12   For You—No Less a Miracle than the Dawn

Streaming through my bedroom window, bright new light.

My eyelids slowly open just in time for this morning's show.

No sign, but assurance of the tree's unwavering devotion.

Greetings.

While pink clouds weave a splendid, steady dance

Through the sleepy whiteness of the early morning sky,

Capturing a fleeting dream-scene, again, my eyelids close.

Moments later, they open again to enjoy a front-row show

Of pink clouds stepping through the stalwart trees.

Flying birds, chirping in concert, sing a hearty hello to all.

Hush. The window stage is ready now to offer its finale.

Low in the eastern sky climbs the long-awaited actor,

One golden glowing ball of light rising each and every day,

The sun intent on warming the whole, wide world.

My every breath in gives thanks and praise, while

Each breath out rings reverence for the miracle display:

Dawn's glorious pageant presented to us each day.

13 Daffodils

Blocking movement,

I clutch guilt in the stillness.

Sobbing,

I delve into the trash of the Past.

Bravely, I discard it all,

Bury it in the compost heap,

Radiant, I look and

Discover daffodils.

14   Anneke's Dance

Dressed in purple, green and yellow,

Skipping around the Maypole,

Tall tree-fairy in springtime,

Greets the day, each stem of grass,

And tiny blossoms new.

Singing *Hallelujah!*

15   Diane, Smiling with the Sun

Diane, smiling with the sun,

Through a field of buttercups,

She's dancing a lazy run.

Hands lifted high,

Holding a butterfly kite,

She's sky-blue, spring-green and buttercup bright.

16   In Spring, the Cherry Tree

In spring, the cherry tree beckons,

I sit down beside it.

A canopy of soft, bunny-pink covering

Caresses me gently,

Warming the last vestiges of winter's cold.

Blossoming umbrella branches hug me

With the warm softness of a mother cradling her newborn baby.

As I sit soaking in the silky view, joy settles over me

Like a small child swinging in the park,

Quietly flying higher into the clear blue sky.

17   When You Smile

In springtime, when you smile,

Streams giggle, lemony-green grass sprouts,

And I unlearn everything.

18   Mountainbird's Song

I'm the mountain bird, aren't I?

I sing and fly.

Nowhere is too high for me.

I soar through the clouds, over treetops and hills.

Still, I need to touch

The earth sometimes,

Perch on a tree branch, and nest,

Be with other birds, and find nourishment that sustains,

Until my next heavenward flight.

FULLNESS

19   Patagonia Love Song

Love. . .

Heals like the doe
Wide-eyed, drinking at the creek,

Startles like tiny cloud tufts
In the desert blue sky,

Refreshes like the spring breeze
Crisp in its caress,

Sparkles like the flower jewel
Purple, yellow, and blue,

Sings like emerald watercress
In the slate blue creek,

Embraces blazing orange-yellow
In the noonday sun,

Soothes at sunset, washing
The sky-island pink, lavender and coral,

Beckons like a lullaby
Promising always

Love. . .

20 God Paints the Sky

I look and see God has been painting again.
When God paints the sky,
I breathe in gold, red.
His vista spreads before me.
He sent the rains.
Raining, raining, will it ever stop? I wonder.
Just what His palette needed.
The dew glistens so intensely.
Then how the colors brighten up His sky.

Across undulating Massachusetts hills, the Creator
Colors my heart with hues
Of grandiose gold, rustic red, and pumpkin orange.
Crisp northern air and woodland beauty, I devour.
I drink, eat, and breathe in tall grasses, trees.
Sky, clouds, friends, and the whispering wind.

Thank you, Lord, for painting the sky today.
No human artist will ever surpass your
masterpiece

That we call *Autumn*.

21   Evening Reverie

Shards of clay
Found in the recesses
Of the mind
Reveal old pictures
Of days in the forest.
The deer dancing
To a waterfall beat.
Hemlock trees reaching from rock outcroppings,
At a ninety-degree angle.
Air so fresh it awakens
Future hopes and dreams
That seem more than possible.

Fishermen in yellow slickers
On a green boat framed within a bright blue sky
Men bemoaning, *No fish yet.*
A rainbow behind them,
Arching above them from hill to hill,.
But, those fools who fail to look back
Miss that treasure.

We laugh and fill our bellies to the
Brim with sweet, harvesttime
Blueberries as big as Alaska boasts.
Quabbin* memories as fine as the sky
With walking trails where waterfalls sing.
We can never go back. . .

But in our reverie
We see, we taste, and the
Recesses of our mind find breezes
Thought lost;

Yet, found tonight in a
Storytime shared by mother and son
Echoes of childhood evening rituals.
Twenty years have passed, but memories
Grow sweeter with time
More precious with age
Like fine wine.

Drink. Drink deep. Life is short
Long,
Trailing like tears
And bubbling like
Merry laughing bells.

*Often, my sons and I took walks to enjoy the wildlife, hills, brooks, and lakes. They grew up by the Quabbin Reservoir in New Salem, Massachusetts. In the 1930's, the former valley with 2,500 residents became a reservoir to supply water to the city of Boston and its surrounding towns.

22   Oh, Mama!

Oh me, oh my, oh Mama!
Giggling still, at 95 years young.
You still flirt with a deftness that I marvel at.
How many people do you know?
And how many have been touched by your smile?

You, so young and beloved,
How can I learn the love of life
You so easily embrace?

How can I live so openly
And follow your lead, Mama?

You willingly forget suffering
And crazy moments; yet,
Still revel in now-new possibilities.
I dance with most amazing you,
While you dance circles around me.

Oh, precious Mama, your arms held wider than the sun,
I embrace your sweet smile, strength, and love.

23   For Johnny, in Memoriam

Sun-heart is your center,

Pure white light surrounds,

Oh, sweet, sweet daisy!

24   A Wedding

In late, hot summer, two lovers, Dorothy and Robert,
Face each other on far ends of the high grass meadow.
They begin a slow, wedding stroll. Then, impatient,
They run to meet in the middle of the field.
With arms lifted high,
They reach through the heavens
To embrace each other.

This outdoor church was designed by an Architect,
Who none can surpass.
Trees are the only walls found at this outdoor church.
No steeple,
But the sun shining in a cloudless, blue, blue sky.
Purple alfalfa, red clover blossoms,
And summertime, rich green grass
Form the thick carpeted floor.
No organ or choir,
But countless birds sing the wedding song.

No wedding guests arrive,
Except God—and a healing wind.
In the middle of the meadow,
They meet to share their wedding vows.
Simple vows: whispers of enduring love and soft
Laughter with promises to share each other's wisdom.

Vows complete,
Dorothy and Robert kiss at the ceremony's close.

This wedding isn't over; it has just begun. . .
Laughing, they form a lazy merry-go-round.
They spin faster and faster,
They hug, breathless and still laughing,
They give thanks and embrace for the
Rest of their lives—and longer.

25   Christmas

Red berries on
The wax-green bush
Bristle bright and
Laughing red.

Snow-sled slides
And horse-drawn rides
Apple-brew and
Pancakes high.

Kiss, my darling.

Yes, we'll fly
To a place
The Lord knows well
Where the Holy Spirit dwells.

Host of angels
Singing clear
Tell all,
Do not fear.

The Lord, your God,
Is drawing near.
Open your heart
And let Him in,

So, this race
You'll surely win.

26 LoveSong

Love is softer than a baby's skin.
    God will show you the way to win.

Love is whiter than fallen snow.
    Angels will block every foe.

Love is slower than the morning rain.
    God will take away your pain.

Love is faster than an ocean wave.
    Jesus will *whosoever* save.

Love is louder than a thunderclap.
    The Bible will show you heaven's map.

27   Perfect Valentine

You are my wonderful Valentine.
Like the stars that, so bright, shine,
You, Father God, light up my life.
You help me in the midst of harrowing strife.
You hold my hand wherever I go.
Answers to my questions, You always know.
Even in my tears, there's always hope.
You promise many joys, so I can cope.
In swirling winds and shifting sand,
You reach down from heaven and hold my hand.
In lonely moments, there's your warm embrace.
Every trial, with **You**, I can face.

Your living Word transforms my mind.
Father God, You **are** my perfect Valentine.

HERSTORY

28 Jewels of Memory

Jewels of memory. . .

Sunny amber of a healing meditation

Sparkling crystal of dancing to a double rainbow arched over the ocean.

Pure diamond of a stranger's smile lighting up a cloudy day.

Heirloom pearl of a newlywed husband shouting in the street,
I love you!

Warm ruby surprise of his body next to mine in the autumn woodland,

And clasped in my heart,

The glorious, sun-moon-star-jewel of

Each newborn gaze of my three sons.

29   The Little Girl Who Dared

Once upon a time, there was a little girl
Who felt all alone in the big, wide world.
She sat on a concrete stoop, waiting for her family to come home,
And when they did, she ate dinner all alone.
At bedtime, upstairs in her room, she covered up her head.
It was so cold and scary in that gigantic bed.
Scuffling sounds of rats running in the night,
Wallpaper demons gave her a very big fright.

Punched and kicked by her big sister and bully boys,
She raced up the hill to school to get away from the noise.
One day, she lost her sister's bracelet while sliding on the ice.
She took it without asking, which was not very nice.
She sobbed and sobbed until she cried a very loud wail.
Frantically, she searched and searched, but to no avail.
And then she was so very late for school
That her teacher hit her hand hard with a wooden rule.

At home, her parents screamed and yelled, night and day,
So, the little girl, in her imagination, would play.
In the yard, she dug in the mud to find a faraway place
Where people spoke softly, hugged and cared.
Maybe, that would happen—if only she dared.
She found a rock and sat down in a little patch of trees
Where God gave her peace—
                              Outside, praying on her knees.

30 My Daughter, Love

Grandfather medicine man is before me chanting
Songs to the Great Spirit.

On the ground, I am crouching over my raven-haired daughter.
Yesterday, smiling, she ran to tell me of sun shining in the water.
In his haste to destroy our village, a US cavalry man
Unknowingly trampled my daughter with his horse.

In her last look, she knew I would protect her against this terror.
Four years with me. Now, she lay under me, no breath left in her.
Nearly all our clan died violent deaths today.
Only the medicine man is left singing praises to our Earth Mother.

Today, I cannot give thanks—my voice is strangled in my throat.
No tears will release this sadness.
No scream will vent anger against this injustice.
The medicine man's healing chant cannot reach across

      The centuries of despair,
             I will
                carry
                    on
                        my
                          back.

31   Toughlove

Two raging males—teenagers too tough for love—
Crowded their anger into a two-room flat,
Lashed out in the streets and at school.
Mother and sons rushed on to a very thin limb
That tore.

And they all went
                    falling,
                         falling
                              andCRASHED.

Then broke into countless, sharp-edged pieces of
Sobbing hearts that hardened into pain-streaked faces.

Fatigued mother, dry-eyed after too-many tears,
Heard God's gentle whisper one frigid winter night,
        Seek, and you will find some Hope sprinkled with Light.
Once cast out, glimmering Faith kept her afloat,
Until cautiously, very cautiously, she tiptoed on the water,
And peered toward faraway shores.
Where the once elongated, lush forest floor now seemed bleak,
black and sparse; yet,
Peering into the distance, under tall majestic trees she spied a
miracle display. . .

One warm blanket of ten thousand blossoms,
Shining yellow, orange, pink, and purple.

32   Missing You

I cannot touch you; memories will have to do.
Crashing, jarring screams—From your nightmare dreams.
Courage and unshed tears—Throughout your many fears.
Marriage never to be; That was your bitter reality.
Elusive job hunt. You put on a brave front.
Trying, trying for normalcy. That was just not to be.
From doctor to doctor, we made the rounds;
Hospitals, therapies, we knew no bounds.
I'm dying. Hospice is needed.
Only a short time I have, you pleaded.
No one could diagnose your ills.
All they did was give you more little pills.
Dutifully, you took them day-by-day,
But they did not help you in any way.
Tormented by sleep that brought no rest.
You tried and tried and did your best.

Seeing your still face the day you died, I cried and cried.
I miss you, darling Tony, my first-born child.

33   The City Trip

Sleeping man, looking very pleased,
Has a deep sleep with warm dreams.
Ten degrees tonight with a wind chill factor of minus twenty.
He lies face up with his head resting on a concrete stoop,
His back flat against the grey, city sidewalk.
He's casually dressed without hat or gloves.
I walk by, careful to not disturb his repose.
A man my age. I cannot just dismiss him.
He's clean and neat, with no scent of alcohol.
His expression that of a man enjoying
The sun in a summer park.

Caught in the swift sidewalk current,
I move on through the blustery streets.

No sauntering tonight. The bitter cold makes my body taut.
My shoulders stiffen in the night freeze.
I'm in a hurry

To get into a warm, cozy building.
Protected by hat, scarf, gloves, and
Winter coat, I am comforted by the promise of a warm bed
And three blanket layers.
I rush on to my destination.
The New York City streets are cold tonight.
No time to ponder this concrete vision.

After the city trip, I return to my country cove.
Two days later, I still shiver, because I'm he and he's me.

I'm still lying on
A grey, concrete mattress
With my head on a grey, concrete pillow.

Will he/me/we awake to this year's spring miracle?

34   *Las Colinas*

Mudslide transformed into smooth, tan-colored ground
As though modern equipment sliced through the jungle.
On each side, little cottages stand untouched
From the top of the hillside down to level ground.
The smooth tan-colored ground cries out. Tears flow
Over the ground watering the hill from the top down
Onto the street and to the other side.
Tears flow with a torrent so strong
It will never end, and we can never forget
Hundreds of people buried forever
Under the tan-colored ground.

Houses deep underneath, where women still stand at their
adobe ovens,
Forever. Children, once playing, laughing and squabbling.
Now, stopped in time.
Under, under, forever, under the tan-colored ground.
Old men discussing the state of the world forever
Ground into the deep. Under forever. Forever under.
Men working, fixing that broken-down truck one more time
For the last time, forever under tan-colored mudslide.
This neighborhood exists now as a torrent of tears.
We who survive cry for our loved ones.

Forever buried under the tan-colored ground.
Crying, crying for El Salvador.
Where are my people who once laughed, cried, ran, sighed?

Under, forever, deep, so deep, we cannot dig them out.
Buried deep under tan-colored ground forever,
Crying out, *Save us. Save our nation.*

El Salvador, El Salvador,
Named after our Lord and Savior.
We need you now, Lord. Save our nation, our people.

Forever in your arms, we want to be—
Not lost under tan-colored ground,

Our lives snuffed out.
We are your People.

Save us, Oh Lord, El Salvador. Help us, now.
Come back, El Señor, Mesías, nuestro Salvador.

Ayúdanos, sálvanos, ahora por favor.
Ahora, El Salvador, nos ayuda, sálvanos.

Note: While on a missionary trip to rebuild a church in El Salvador, our bus passed by the *Las Colinas* neighborhood of *Santa Tecla*. On January 13, 2001, El Salvador suffered from hundreds of earthquakes that resulted in many deaths. The 7.7 magnitude earthquake, caused a massive landslide in Las Colinas, causing an estimated 585 deaths. It left a huge yellow-brown swatch of ground in the landscape, that became a terrible burial ground for those who died that day.

(Landslides Triggered by the 13 January 2001. . . Earthquakes. . . Randall Gibson et al. USGS. Index ID 70217356. 2004.)

35   Secrets Sea Salt Sings

Once at the shore, sea salt sinks into each membrane.

Releasing pockets of blockages that time has thickened into regrets.

Breezes ruffle bedcovers of my anxious thoughts.

Waves dance in undulating roll, singing rounds of mellifluous melodies,

Murmuring like soft honey-lipped kisses.

Winds shake the wrinkles off dusty weariness.

Palms and belly press down, gently mooring into the soothing sand.

Giggling, shouting, and running footsteps become faint as

Drowsiness drops down into dreams I cannot remember.

Asleep on a tiny towel transformed into an island refuge

Where, forever now, only wonder exists where waves

Crash into the shore and. . .

Life is easy. There are flower petals in my slippers and

The storytime butler brings me breakfast.

Hey, hey, the waves. . . Voices crash into my slumber.

Then I feel a wet nibble at my toes and giggle at love's sensual play.

Hey. Hey, a warning cry I hear dimly, my eyes flutter open like butterfly wings.

The sun floods brightly into eyes that peek open,

Herstory

As high tidewater waves crash into the shore and

Sea salt water tingles, taunts, tickles toes, teasing laughter from me. I jump up.

Over my shoulder, I look back to see sea salt waves stilled by time.

Running like a deer who jumps over the guardrail,

In a staggering race to the other side. Still

Inside the dream, I grab fistfuls of towel refuge, book, beach bag. . .

Tried to warn you, coaxes the handsome man, a grin wide with welcome.

Semi-conscious, I smile, automatically mumbling quiet gratitude.

Higher on the shore, I anchor on towel island--drop down to dreaming again.

Awakening later, I look back at sea salt waves,

Rolling in an undulating high-tide dance that

Wakens others slumbering in summer beach delight.

Melodious waves incessantly murmur soft kisses on my earlobe.

Like a confident lover, they shake off cobwebs, brush off bruises of the day,

Unravel sleep snags while renewing like a freshly-made bed.

Sharp images captured into no-time. Billowing clouds in a sky brand-new blue.

Softly, God's breath whispers secrets, while sea salt sings.

36   The Healing Circle

The angels had a meeting
And this is what they said,
Instead of tea for our celebration,
Why not a cup of love instead?

The angels started looking for a ball of light to throw.
Once one angel found one, she threw it to the next.
It went 'round and 'round the circle
Until the night lit up like day.

The angels had this meeting
They gathered 'round to heal—
People who were weary and in a lot of pain.
The people kept on coming until the hall was very full.

Soon too-many tears were falling from each and every eye. The people
felt life was a struggle and worried from day to night.
But, then, they started celebrating with the angels in that healing hall.
Each drank in the love and bounced that light around.

At that very moment, right in that great, grand hall,
A marvelous healing mist had just begun to fall.
The tears that had been flowing turned into a warm and gentle rain.
That showered over all the worries and carried them far away.

The people marveled at their healing,
The cleansing rain and the night lit up like day.
But the first angel shook her head and responded with a gentle sigh,
This miracle is just a tiny fragment of what God's love can do.

To close the evening meeting, they joined in a midnight toast,
The angels and the people lifted up their love-full cups.
The first angel gave the toast that echoed throughout the hall,
For all of you, blessings in every moment and marvels in every day anew.

They all kissed and hugged with love still overflowing.
To end their perfect meeting and bid everyone adieu,
The angels and the people held hands in a giant spiral
That circled upward from that hall and reached right into heaven.

Then, they all sang a song as bright as a new moon star.
Each glorious note of their singing went floating on the wind:
A wind that whispered in people's hearts all around the world,
Especially sleeping infants, who stirred in their beds and smiled.

ABOUT THE POET

Mountainbird

This collection of poems emerged over the course of twenty years. Just as, after much struggle, a chrysalis emerges from its cocoon to become a beautiful butterfly, Mountainbird metamorphosed from an insecure, emotionally distraught young adult to a more peaceful, yet still evolving, maturity. However, her entrance into adult life began in a **Cocoon** of despair.

Through experiences that developed **Awakening**, her trials and tribulations culminated in a love of joy that life can bring—and a more hesitant appreciation for the inevitable strife.

Encompassing **Fullness**, she transitioned from full-time motherhood to graduate studies. After eight years of study, while single-parenting three sons, she entered the full-time workforce with a doctorate in hand. However, success in creative and educational avenues did not exempt Mountainbird from personal crisis or tragedy.

In **Herstory**: she relates a personal history of travels, empty nesting, grief after her first-born son's death, and joy in nature's beauty. Reluctantly, slowly, she embraces the fullness of life that includes its crises, heart-wrenching grief, and amazing joys.

Journey with her as you read her poems. As a newly divorced young mother, she began a timid start as an author when she tossed her first poetry submission into an old-fashioned post office box on the side of a country road. After she threw her letter in, she quickly shut the lid, so she could not change her mind. Thus, Mountainbird's published writing journey began with the poem, *By a New Salem Brook during Midwinter's Thaw,* first published in the small, country town newsletter, *The Wendell Times* of Wendell, Massachusetts. As the years passed, she published poems, scholarly articles, educational manuals, local newspaper columns, and (eventually) books.

Her first book *is Lookin' Up in Down Times: Stars Shine Bright on a Moonless Night.* Her second is a children's picture book, *The Healing Circle. Mountainbird Melodies: Book One—Dances with Waterfalls* is her third book.

Mountainbird

ABOUT THE ARTIST

Lydia Noble

At just 12 years old, Lydia Noble's first venture into professional art began when she embarked on illustrating this book. Her parents, Paul and Heather Noble, cannot recall a time that Lydia was not drawing. Over her short lifetime, she had hardly ever shown her parents any of the hundreds of art projects that she diligently worked on. After completing her home-schooling work each day, Lydia would draw and paint to her heart's content.

Lydia rose to the challenge as illustrator; first, by simply allowing another to see her work and; second, by accomplishing the demanding work of revision. Illustration of *Mountainbird Melodies Book One—Dances with Waterfalls* entailed going back and forth with the writer, who had her unique vision for the cover and sections of the book. The challenge for the writer is how to communicate something visual without the drawing skills of the artist. However, the young artist was up to the challenge. Without hesitation, Lydia dove into each revision with the utmost grace and, even, enthusiasm.

Lydia Noble is a student of art, ballet, quilting, nature, and all things beautiful. She is inspired by her faith and by the unique coastal scenery of eastern North Carolina where she resides. *Mountainbird Melodies: Book One—Dances with Waterfalls* is her first experience as a book illustrator. She genuinely hopes her artwork blesses and encourages others on their journey.

Lydia, at the beginning of this journey.

ENDNOTES

In a public reading, a poet often offers a short introduction before each poem.
These *ENDNOTES* are for the curious.

COCOON

The **COCOON** section embraces a time of insecurity and pain. As a young adult
and new mother, winter in the Northeast U.S.A. often brought bouts of
depression. In many transitions from town to city and town again, from
apartments to rental houses with many goodbyes came feelings of deep
loneliness. I felt so insecure and unloved. Constantly, I looked for and yearned for,
love. At my core, I wanted life to be perfect.

1 Instant Anything Wouldn't we all like to change our circumstances without the
work?

2 January Oh, how the cold and darkness of winter depressed me.

3 Bowl Full of Cherries In my young adult and young married life, I moved over
14 times. Finally, I got tired of the boxes, moving trucks, new neighborhoods,
finding new friends and, most of all, the continual goodbyes.

4 *Someday* and *Maybe* A first relationship after a painful divorce was full of angst
and devoid of clear communication. Though I had neither words nor
understanding of PTSD at that time, my friend was a Vietnam veteran who
suffered terribly. He showed both a desire and fear of getting close. As a recently
divorced, insecure, and naïve woman, his demeanor was very confusing. This
fledgling relationship marked the beginning of a long, arduous learning process.

5 Circles What a wonderful world it would be if. . .

6 Fear of Flying About an infatuation with a wild, crazy, fearless cowboy.

7 Wooing Wind The constant desire for more in life.

8 Beckoning Beyond As a recently divorced mother of young boys who grew into rebellious teens, life felt harrowing at times. Somehow, I would muster up a glimmer of light and hopefulness. Thankfully, later they matured into kind, courteous, responsible young men.

9 Stars in the Night Each painful experience led me closer and closer to God. in my darkest moments, I would desperately cry out and pray to God for help, and, somehow, He always answered me with peace.

AWAKENING

The ***AWAKENING*** section reflects a growing healing process. Being in nature always was, and still is, my peaceful place. I began to experience God in a more personal way. Winter in northeastern Massachusetts was always hard, but spring came with hope, flowers, and new life. My newfound passion was pottery. While learning to center on the wheel, slowly I began to center myself. I joined Dance Spree. Dance Spree was held in a huge room with a wooden floor. Everyone took off their shoes and just danced freely alone, with one or two others, or free formed groups. During this ***Awakening***, I began to lose many fears I had held on to my entire life.

10 By a New Salem Brook at Midwinter's Thaw The Quabbin Reservoir offered miles and miles of woodland where I could walk leisurely, often stopping to hear the melody created by brooks as the water rushed over the rocks.

11 The Potter's Dance A lighthearted look at the potter at the potter's wheel.

12 For You—No Less a Miracle than the Dawn I wrote this for Dawn, a young college student who disliked her name. I created the poem as a gift to her, hoping she would discover the beauty of her name.

13 Daffodils Don't the springtime yellow daffodils speak to us?

14 Anneke's Dance Reflections on Anneke's dance at Dance Spree in Northampton, Massachusetts.

15 Diane, Smiling with the Sun Another dancer at Dance Spree.

16 In Spring, the Cherry Tree After a long harsh winter in northwestern Massachusetts, the spring season is full of blossoms and promise.

FULLNESS

This ***FULLNESS*** section reflects a growing maturity in emotions, thought and experience. While these poems are not really chronological, they describe moments and events, where I began to embrace, not just the joys, but also the times of despair. Throughout, I marvel at God's creation, which includes nature and His people.

HERSTORY

The ***HERSTORY*** section includes some of the poet's life stories—true events, whether literal, visionary or metaphorical.

28 Jewels of Memory Inspired by treasured memories of my three sons, romance, and my newly-wed husband's unabashed love.

29 The Little Girl Who Dared A harkening back to a childhood of hurt and shame. Faith was and is my salvation. I first shared this poem at an interdenominational New Year's Eve event at Global River Church in Wilmington, North Carolina.

30 My Daughter, Love During a prayer meeting, I experienced a Native American vision, which became the inspiration for this poem.

31 Toughlove Being a single mom of three teens was a hard, sharp-edged place.

32 Missing You Oh, how I grieved the loss of my first-born son when he was only 33 years old.

33 The City Trip For about two decades, I lived in the small country town of New Salem, population of about 600. During a New York City trip with the Massachusetts Dance Spree group, I became acutely aware of the homeless population. What a shock to see so many sitting and lying on the sidewalks on that subfreezing evening.

34 *Las Colinas* On my first short-term international mission trip to El Salvador, I saw this wide, bare swatch of land on the hillside between rows of neighborhood cottages and asked what it was. I learned about a series of earthquakes. In a matter of minutes, almost 600 people died when they were buried alive in a mudslide.

35 Secrets Sea Salt Sings This was my first of many gorgeous experiences at Wrightsville Beach, North Carolina. It literally was the calm before the storm. When I tried to return the next day, the road was closed in readiness for a major hurricane.

36 The Healing Circle After years of not attending any church, I found Hope Community Church in Amherst, Massachusetts. When Pastor LaVerne spoke, I knew he was genuine when he said, each day, he walked with his best friend, the Lord. In that tiny multicultural, nondenominational church, I returned to my spiritual roots, Christianity. A few of us met each Monday evening to pray for others. We stood in a circle and prayed for each person who sat in a chair in the middle. This poem is my vision of what happens as we pray. The creation of this poem was inspired by a desire to present a birthday gift to and my love for my spiritual father, the anointed Pastor LaVerne Anderson. I stayed up all night reciting aloud over and over, while writing and rewriting. For Pastor LaVerne, I pushed through my overwhelming fear to recite this poem aloud in front of the birthday gathering of about 100 people. More than 30 years later, this poem inspired me to produce my first children's picture book, *The Healing Circle*, which depicts a group of angels and people as diverse as those who attended that little church.

POEMS *PREVIOUSLY PUBLISHED*

Copyright of all poems remains with Mountainbird.

By a New Salem Brook at Midwinter's Thaw. First published in the Wendell Post, Wendell, Massachusetts. Circa 1982.

My Daughter, Love. First published in Agana, Guam, *Hafa.* February 1991. Vol. III, No. 2, p. 32.

You—No Less a Miracle Than the Dawn. First published in Agana, Guam, *Hafa.* February 1991. Vol. III, No. 2, p. 32.

Other previously published poems. *Patagonia Love Song.* Circa 1997. *God Paints the Sky.* Circa 1988.

The Healing Circle. First reading for Reverend LaVerne Anderson at Hope Community Church, Amherst, Massachusetts. Circa 1986.

Published in book format for the children's book of the same name, *The Healing Circle* by Mountainbird ©1986 original poem. © 2017 Hardback book version. ISBN. 978-1-7347363-0-2. Light Messages in the U.S.A. Also, find publications in paperback, e-book and bilingual English/Spanish and English/French versions.

Mountainbird with Lydia Noble.

"As I sit soaking in the silky view, joy settles over me
Like a small child swinging in the park,
Quietly flying higher into the clear blue sky."

From *In Spring, the Cherry Tree* by Mountainbird.
Art by Lydia Noble.

www.ingramcontent.com/pod-product-compliance
Lightning Source LLC
Chambersburg PA
CBHW030824060726
47590CB00004B/1386